THE COINCIDENCE OF CASTLES

The Coincidence of Castles
Copyright © 2014 Tobi Cogswell
Paperback ISBN: 978-1-941783-01-6

All rights reserved: except for the purpose of quoting brief passages for review, no part of this book may be reproduced or transmitted in any form or by any means, electronic or mechanical, including photocopying, recording, or by any information storage and retrieval system, without permission in writing from the publisher.

Cover photo: Jeffrey C. Alfier
Cover design: Steven Asmussen
Design & Layout: Steven Asmussen
Copyediting: Elizabeth Nichols

Glass Lyre Press, LLC.
P.O. Box 2693
Glenview, IL 60026

www.GlassLyrePress.com

THE COINCIDENCE OF CASTLES

POEMS OF IRELAND

TOBI COGSWELL

Acknowledgements

Grateful acknowledgement is made to the following journals in which these poems originally appeared, or are forthcoming, sometimes in a slightly different format

Chiron Review
"A Slip Away at Crookhaven Marina"
"Widower Beattie Brings a Woman Home"

Driftwood Press
"The Man Steps into Nettles on the Way to Mass"

Hobo Camp Review
"Soft Enquiry of Morning"

Pea River Journal
"Inishbofin"

Penumbra
"Erected by James MacDonald, Loving Husband"

POEM
"Evening of Island Grace"

Poppy Road Review
"The Meeting"

Prole
"Annie at the City Center Pub"

Red River Review
"The Coincidence of Castles"
"The Sorceress of Galway Bay"

Third Wednesday
"At the Park Hotel"

Town Creek Poetry
"How Hate Returned to Love at Wexford Harbour"

Welter
"Suitcase"

Contents

Suitcase	11
At the Park Hotel	12
Wisdom and Water	13
Annie at the City Center Pub	14
The Man Steps into Nettles on the Way to Mass	15
Soft Enquiry of Morning	16
The Meeting	17
Trawler's Gauntlet	18
A Slip Away at Crookhaven Marina	19
Evening of Island Grace	20
How Hate Returned to Love at Wexford Harbour	21
The Coincidence of Castles	22
Erected by James MacDonald, Loving Husband	23
Widower Beattie Brings a Woman Home	24
The Sorceress of Galway Bay	25
Shadow and Quay	26
Inishbofin	27
Saturday Evening at Murray's Bar	28
Mapping the Boundaries, Sharing the Sky	29
Homeward	30
About the Poet	33

To Men of Worth, and to Jeff, without whom Ireland would have seemed a very different place.

Suitcase

Must carry the green and brown boiled wool
of a sweater, old as a castle floor in ghostlight,
picked from the pile of "going to nobody's," the scent
of home enough to keep you gone and bring you back.

Must be small and square enough to carry, to carry pens
and books and how to write the checkerboard of country
as it gives way to the blue-black of oceans, cities full of life
we can only imagine and cannot understand.

Must gracefully negotiate rutted tracks, manicured lawns,
the gravel crush of footpaths to a resting place, days
or weeks, with pockets to hold secrets and silences,
a note that wraps its arms around your vagrant heart.

At the Park Hotel
Shannon, Ireland

The Saturday night band plays
fiddle and forgiveness in the pub
in the airport hotel. The innocents
are deaf, watch rugby on the TV

behind the bar, think about tomorrow's
business. His chapped fingers read her face
as she leans into them, across a small table
just enough for two chairs and locked eyes.

Her wedding ring is in her pocket.
His is miles away on a dresser
that used to be filled with silks and sachets,
now empty as a beachfront at dawn.

The maps are in their minds. She wants
to be moaned pretty and he just wants.
Shadows slip through stone—
the stories, this room, these walls.

Soft breathing of *we will choose
not to remember this tomorrow,*
the gray morning sky turning pink,
fringing the world in defiant blush.

Wisdom and Water

She closes her jet lagged eyes,
vertigo rocks her gently to dream-riddled
sleep of lichened boats, horses, and music
playing in soft language she can't pronounce.

Hilly, rocky land slopes to the movement
of ancient growth of islands, green and gray
sandwiched between the two blues
of sky and sea.

And in the farthest reaches of her dream,
a fisherman—a face familiar as time,
but she does not know him. He is her father,
her brother, her lover. He provides. She sleeps.

Annie at the City Center Pub

She is a hillside woman.
Part faerie, part pied piper
she lifts her toasts to each
work hardened farmer
and fisherman in City Center Pub,
Friday evenings, no matter
if wind is haunting the purple
blossoms up horse-trekked paths
or the sky is lamb-docile and quiet.

She leaves and they follow,
not to sneak a kiss nor steal a touch,
but to abide a bit longer with her as she says
goodnight to another leather-warped day,
make silent prayer for a heartening morrow.

This is the church of seabirds
and saints. A final bow to the tides
sends the men to their wives,
to soup in the kettle and bread
that needs breaking. To ruddy-cheeked
child-fellows stopping to scrape
the day's stink from their shoes, fist
a handful of wildflowers before
going to girls who will soon
be their wives.

Whiskey and heather, stone and lace,
her day is done. Back at her room
above the pub, shadows from streetlights
fountain like hair down her back as she takes
down the pins, takes down her stockings,
and waits for the sound of the current, the smell
of the moon, to toast her—just her,
to breathe their goodnights.

The Man Steps into Nettles on the Way to Mass

Dressed in his "church pants," he cuts through a field
like a rabbit on skates. Late as he often is, he'll get "the eye"

from some chuntering old usher—get nothing but grief
from postman to pub to his mother and wife,

who left ahead of him–early–gently walking the road,
the sway of her contentment like a velvet metronome.

Sometimes they walk together—he pestering the edges
of her hair with bawdy words that pink her cheeks,

that she'll remember later, after family obligations
and a quick snippet of cake allow for their own time,

curtains pulled to shadows, a vase of yellow on the table
and the two of them, a rippled alchemy of lust and love.

But not today. And now the nettles, thick around his legs
like fire ants, pay him back for being slothful,

one of his sins. He will sit toward the back and pray
for the sting to dissolve in the distance, his whispered psalm.

Soft Enquiry of Morning

He wakes too early on Saturday morning,
last night's pub celebration clamoring
smack between two furrowed brows.

Thinking man's brows can judge the sea
with merely a glance, to know if the traps
are full, if there will be money tonight.

I need a smoke, he thinks, cracks a can
of anything lager to take the edge off,
looks back in his sheets to the sleeping

cello of naked woman, her back turned
toward him, her face turned so that sky
will be what she sees on fluttering awake.

The failed garden outside brings a scent
of yeasty mildew—it's that time of year
and he does not work the land.

Street sounds bellow inside his head
as he touches the curve of her hip.
This is a small town, and she is a small-town

woman. No promises given, none received.
Paths map the fog that will hold their silence,
the gray dawn, a confessional, absolves their sin.

The Meeting

Buy me a ticket on the morning ferry,
meet me at the quay. I have just a small bag—
don't be disappointed. We don't even know
if we can dance this dance.

Stop at the shop, buy apples, brown bread,
good butter, better coffee. I know you
already have the wine, brought over
from your earlier trip to Barcelona.

I will be wearing a blouse—
the lightest pink of your imagination.
My hair will be damp, face flushed
from anticipation and the crested sea.

Hold me as if I were your lifesaver.
The strength of your arms will write whether
I leave on the next tide, whether the ghosts
of morning breezes ensure we survive.

Trawler's Gauntlet

The sea's wide indifference echoes the gray of brackish sky.
Nowhere do tides channel the moodiness of a bored, changeless
moon more than here. Even hidden by cloud, by weather,

by the faithfulness of daylight, the moon is an ever-present ghost.
Horizons dissolve in the damp maritime air while strident tides
offer a peep-show of land between two islands, or hide it,

like a Victorian woman showing a comely ankle before spiriting it away,
a demon whose invitation to drown goes unnoticed until too late.
The tides drop the lace of their skirted curtains

in the blink of a wary barkeep's eye. Best to be inside, under
his protected roof, or know the decay that will be your boat,
know the legend that will be yours, a cross and a crystal.

A Slip Away at Crookhaven Marina

The low rumble of a party below decks,
bad guitar and awkward laughter.
Shadows as women in tank tops
and teased hair flit past lit portholes.
The rest of the marina empty or dream-silent.

I listen to the tiptoe of easy rain,
wait for sleep. The odd engine
a white noise more drumbeat
than soothing, and the tide going out.

I stretch, touch both walls cradling
the bow-bed with fingertips and feet—
what usually brings comfort, tonight
could smother. I know the change
of light by the smell of sea.

The party just a mumble now,
a chord strummed here and there
in time with the outbound ferry.
The soft song of shorebirds
as they shake off early mist
and evening drizzle. Soon, the bare
grey light of northern morning.

I pull the covers tight and try a little longer
for dreams not of salt or sky, but touch.
There is no forgiveness in the oars of a small
boat heading ashore, wood to water
with calm deliberation.

This will be a tousled hair,
don't meet their eyes kind of day.
It has been ordained, as waves
tumble relentless through hollowed stone.

Evening of Island Grace

The moon owns the harbor tonight.
I carry it large and bright in my mind

as I drift up the headlands to have
a lover's view. The tranquil quiet

of sleeping vessels—by day they perform
all sorts of feats, from fishing, to rescue,

to the connection of families, some
long away and some only to the mainland

for the dentist and a pint. Now the calm skiffs
and trawlers, tugs and ferries sleep

in a sanctuary lodged firmly in my heart.
The rusted mooring rings embedded in the quay

are part of me. I dream the silvered splash
of nighttime life we never see, watch the gentle

call from one bird to its mate, his brilliant red
invisible in blackened sky, smell the ovens

planning for a morning of toast and tea.
I am alone in the hours before breaking light

but have never been so full—my arms wrap around
the chorus of ocean. It sings my heart shoreward.

How Hate Returned to Love at Wexford Harbour

They never finished their wild conversation, ghostly
howls of murderous wind cutting off all but the sight—
violet colors, a seastorm of rage between them.

Dark eyes narrowed, holding each other hostage
in the deepening night. Shoulders formed rocky
and stoic promontories against the seawall,

which held stubborn against their passionate shouts.
And when rivulets of mist and tears grew dense enough
to weigh, turned to sky meeting churning sea, when cobblestones

became the harbour floor—they could either choose to stand down,
or spend forever hating themselves for hating each other.
Their choice was made. The heat of clenched fists

became a hearth. A touch to a collarbone, bared,
safe from the thundersquall roiling along the quay,
became a sigh of all things right and true.

And now, when ravens own the night, fog corks
the lighthouse, and not a bicycle or drunk is fumbling
home in blinded streets, at one house lives tranquility.

The Coincidence of Castles

Stone by stone
a fortress
stacked with grace
through bloodied seasons.

The smell of peat,
the smoke of dreams
forgotten, remembered,
no one is let down.

A row of red brick
level above the window.
Plaster ceiling chunking down
on uneven hidden stairs.

Surround yourself with sages
of all burning hues.
Look to the eventuality
of lavender and daffodils,

sweetness and armor.
As long as I've loved you
I have roamed this place,
six centuries and more.

Erected by James MacDonald, Loving Husband

Come sit here beside me
skin lit, a candle
on alabaster, small gold rings
draw my eyes to your neck
your pulse beating, hands still.

It has always been like
the first time. The first kiss,
first lovemaking, first
child. The children.

Your smile never died,
even as we both grew older,
less able to sway with the wind
of disappointments and sadnesses.

I still see you in your
wedding veil, the one
our daughters also wore, being
both poor in material riches
and also superstitious.

I drink to you in the glass
you loved so well—the sun
piercing reddened shadows
on the wall above your empty chair.

My heart. It will not be long
until we dance again,
eyes bright,
fingers straight and sure.
'Til we marvel at the golden
blossoms along emerald hills,
and what takes the place of sky.
Save a place for me.
I will not find another.

Widower Beattie Brings a Woman Home

Respect and longing were two sides of Beattie's coin,
like dark rain that ripens storm clouds waiting for light.
He looked across fields carpeted with blanket-softness
and remembered why he loved her when she slept.
A sigh, a celebration, a cathedral of human hungers—
It was time.

Quite low-key, Beattie was. A walk, a meeting
of eyes, an umbrella proffered under a sky rich with weather.
Where he walks a door opens, a chance meeting,
a delicate vision with calm hands and smooth hair
enters the fog just ahead of him. Their shadows dance
on cobbled streets lit by flickering lamps.

They have many polite conversations over time
as they both walk toward the sea, a place for thought
and contemplation. He touches her face
like a blind man reaching for shooting stars.
She points to something just over the horizon.
They let the wind carry them.

The Sorceress of Galway Bay

She feels music in her body.
Graceful as a thousand ships
set off to sail, she rocks gently,
toe tapping, sometimes heel
striking exclamations in a
sad lament or spirited reel.

Her face, calm as sea birds gliding
in an updraft, pale against
the blues and grays; so her
lace scarf sits about her neck.
And when she sings, she looks
at everyone, just a fraction

of connection. Men remember how
they used to crave their wives—
8th notes flutter, cheeks turn pink,
pearl buttons on a concertina
make promises to surely be kept,
before this sweet night sleeps.

Shadow and Quay

A rare morning—
the remnants of moon crosshatch the pillow
on which her husband sleeps. She listens for the calm breath
that means he is traveling somewhere lovely in dream.
She touches his hand, he holds hers instinctively.

An unusual May dawn, the breeze floats through curtains
open to the peaceful day. She smells hearth smoke
rising from her neighbor's house, hears the morning birds—
the far off sound of steady song, a mockingbird nearby,
and always, the sea.

Soon she will know the place on the quay that scents
of rusted anchorage. She will watch the shadow
of storms against roughened plaster, she will see
the metronome ticking out the rhythm to a Celtic fiddle song,
but she will not hear any of it.

And so this dawn, she memorizes her peaceful man,
imagines where the birds have led him. She quiets
and treasures her own breath, where breath and heart
form a chapel. Where the music of remembrance is made,
where it will never be forgotten.

Inishbofin
for Donnie, James and Bronagh

This is an island owned by wind,
with whistling chimneys and blowing
grasses. Where the blues and blacks
of the bay offer commerce, and the odd plaque
of tragedy—sea against somebody's son.

Where the priest rides the ferry on Saturday.
An afternoon sermon ensures return to his own
congregation for Sunday. Where flowers explode
purple and gold, and clothes blow sideways on lines.

Where a climb atop any hill views water, sheep
and horses bony as life-sized pebbles.
A strengthened resolve to best any hardship,
and many a story to prove it—in the pub, in the fields.
Guinness on draught and coal in the bucket.

A quiet island until you listen.
A family island, with stories of other families,
other islands, and how they all came to be here.
How they stay. Strong men and dear women.
They sing about leaving but they stay.
Now you have tea with their children,
watch their little ones in oiled jackets and rubber boots.

The boats. Trace the embossing on a ruined skiff
to learn it is named after a saint, not a woman.
The barns. Tin ceilings blind in today's sun,
tomorrow they will play concertos in unforgiving rain.
The textures. Rocky, boggy. The corner of a house
worn away to reveal stone, the same stone that borders fields.
Cotton and clover. The dry brown of striped paths
through green. The dry brown of outbound tide.

A wondrous island. Bone-chilling cold, but still well-mannered
and welcoming. They sing about leaving but they stay.

Saturday Evening at Murray's Bar

The hours advance into the quiet grace of failing light.
Four musicians tune up. Guitar, fiddle, banjo…
the same hands that pluck the strings of the mandolin
touch her thigh lightly, as if in secret, the words
of the ballads in a dialect known only to her.

Curtains of rain shadow streetlights. Watermarks of amber
shelter cars, lovers caught outside for a quick smoke,
a shuttered farmhouse far afield, and the ever-present sheepdog,
on call, searching for his last remaining wards, their
presence camouflaged by dark, and the smell of winter.

Gleaming faces, shining eyes crosshatched from shadows
thrown by the fire, amplified by excitement as the first notes
are tentatively played, and pints are lifted. Nowhere to dance,
though high heels and boots alike tap a gauntlet thrown, a dare
to kiss the rhythm of intimacy, the caress of island harmonies.

Mapping the Boundaries, Sharing the Sky

Cleggan has a Texas sky today, a wary countenance,
her horizon dissolved in a wash of squinting distance.
In Texas the mountains stand so far beyond,
they seem like islands wearing a frayed sleeve of sun.
In Cleggan they *are* islands, far and full of story.

There's a common blue heaven swollen with dirty cloud.
It waits for the crosshatch of rain to resound over fields,
rutted and boundaried with local rock, the work
of summer sons and back-bent fathers.
Texas storms vanish telephone wires, pump-jacks,

lines marking the two-way, the daring resolve
of a trucker leaning toward home, toward his woman,
or somebody else's woman, who keeps a frayed seat
waiting at the bar, quarters ready for the jukebox
and a soft hand to wipe the warm sweat from his cold glass.

Rumor has it that pirate Grace O'Malley carried knives.
Wild woman with hair of lust and heartbreak, she carved
many a tattoo on soldier and slave. Texas women nod to her
memory when tucking daggers—a quick slice marks
faster than a Peregrine catches prey, and they will do it.

Cleggan is a Texas sister today. Lie in the scent of ozone
and sea. Watch shorebirds volley through dusky light.
Greet silent hawks as they climb over cutbank
and willow. Green is green anywhere, but a Texas sky
is scarcely shared. And daggers rarely seen.

Homeward

At the end of a millennium-weary multi-textured pier,
stacked water to walking-quay with buckets and creels
stands the pub.

You enter from a walkway of polished river stones
to the scent of local chowder and dark wood,
a pool table and posters for ales extinct before your birth.

You barely notice the bus at the corner, cars rushing by
on its other side. A fair likeness of the Interstate waiting
to carry you south to the next town you hope welcomes you.

Bread and soup later, a pint of Harp for balance,
you head toward the bus, climb into its weathered splendor,
focus out the window—your task to remember

those things for which there is no time to take a photograph.
Such green. So much decrepit beauty. A living Gothic romance.
Wildly hanging moss climbs on shells of buildings barely visible

at lake-edge, hawks grace the sky. The bus threads its straight,
modern path. You are poised one foot in the past, one in the future,
afraid to blink, unwilling to leave even one memory behind.

GLASS LYRE PRESS, LLC
"Exceptional works to replenish the spirit"

Poetry collections
Poetry chapbooks
Select short & flash fiction
Anthologies

Glass Lyre Press is an independent literary publisher interested in technically accomplished, stylistically distinct, and original work. Glass Lyre seeks diverse writers that possess a dynamic aesthetic, and an ability to emotionally and intellectually engage a wide audience of readers.

Glass Lyre's vision is to connect the world through language and art. We hope to expand the scope of poetry and short fiction for the general reader through exceptionally well-written books, which evoke emotion, provide insight, and resonate with the human spirit.

www.GlassLyrePress.com